Up in Space

Sun and Moon

Rosalind Mist

QED Publishing

Editor: Lauren Taylor
Designer: Melissa Alaverdy
Educational consultants:
   Heather Adamson
   and Jillian Harker

Copyright © QED Publishing,
2013

First published in the UK by
QED Publishing,
A Quarto Group Company
230 City Road,
London EC1V 2TT

www.qed-publishing.co.uk

ISBN 978 1 78171 214 6

Printed in China

A catalogue record for this
book is available from the
British Library.

Picture credits
(fc=front cover, t=top,
b=bottom, l=left, r=right,
c=centre)

Getty Images Michal Cizek
10-11
NASA David R. Scott 18-19,
22-23, 23t
Science Photo Library
NASA/GSFC-SVS 1b, Detlev
Van Ravenswaay 4b, 13t,
NASA/GSFC-SVS 1b16-17
Shutterstock 1t, Paul Fleet
2-3, 4-5, 6-7, Pakhnyushcha
8-9, Mahesh Patil 9t, Paul
Fleet 12-13, Missanzi 14,
Xtremer 14-15, Molodec 15b,
EpicStockMedia 16-17, 20b,
Myotis 21, Triff 24

Words in bold appear in the
Glossary on page 24.

Contents

What is the Sun?

The Sun is a very hot, huge ball. It is made of burning gas.

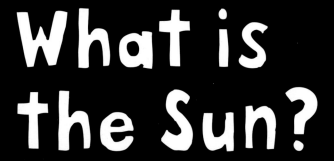

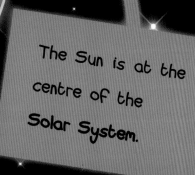

The Sun is at the centre of the Solar System.

4

The Solar System

The Solar System is made up of the Sun and all the things that go around it. Planets and their **moons** are part of this system. So are comets, asteroids and meteors.

Sun

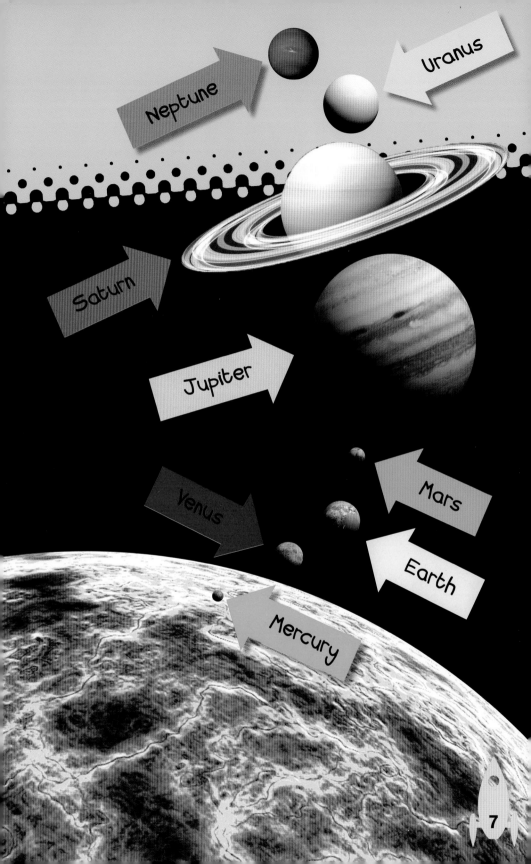

Neptune

Uranus

Saturn

Jupiter

Mars

Venus

Earth

Mercury

7

Sunlight

The Sun makes light that shines on the Earth. The Sun shines on one side of the Earth. It is day on this side.

daylight

It is night on
the dark side.

Rainbows

Sunlight is made
of seven colours.
Sometimes sunlight passes
through raindrops. Then a
rainbow forms.

All seven colours form an arch across the sky.

Stormy Sun

The Sun makes heat
too. The middle
of the Sun is the
hottest part.

The burning gases
make great storms
of fire.

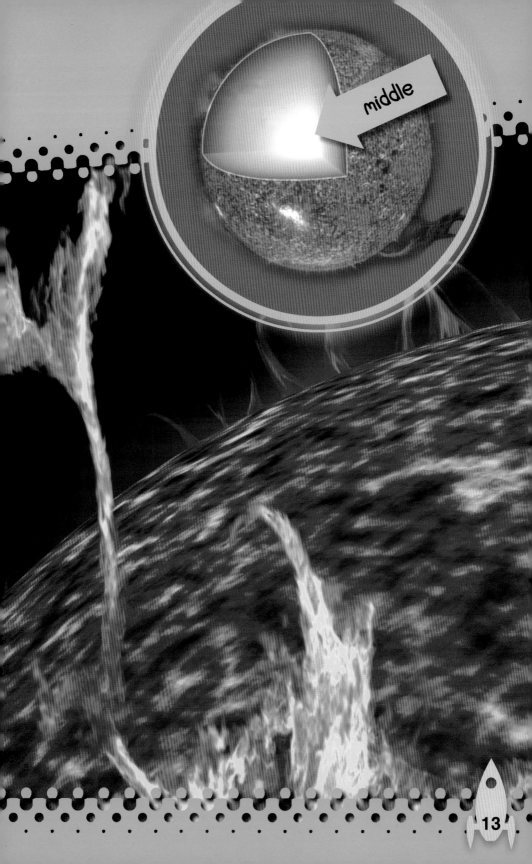

middle

Solar eclipse

Sometimes the Moon moves between the Sun and the Earth. It blocks the Sun's light. It becomes dark just like night-time. This is called a **solar eclipse**.

Earth

Sun

Moon

solar eclipse

The Moon

The Moon is a round, rocky ball that goes around the Earth. It is made of pale rocks. The rocks reflect light from the Sun.

The Moon is the brightest object in the night sky.

Craters

Sometimes rocks from space crash into the Moon. They make holes called **craters**.

Some craters are so wide that a large city could fit inside them.

craters

Full moon, half moon

The Moon seems to change shape. This is because the Sun lights up different parts. Sometimes the Moon looks round. Then it is called a full moon.

full moon

Sometimes you can see only half the circle. Then it is called a half moon.

Flying to the Moon

The Moon is about 385,000 kilometres away. **Astronauts** travelled there in fast **rockets.**

the Moon

rocket

If you could drive
a car to the Moon,
it would take
over 4 months
to get there!

Glossary

astronaut – someone who travels in space

crater – a hole in the ground caused by something falling or by a volcano

moon – a natural object that moves around a planet

planet – one of the eight large objects circling the Sun

rainbow – an arc of colours caused by sunlight shining through water droplets

rocket – a vehicle with a powerful engine that can launch objects into space

solar eclipse – a time when the Moon comes between the Sun and the Earth so that all or part of the Sun's light is blocked

Solar System – the Sun and all of the things that move around it

Sun – the star that the Earth and the planets move around